# Transforming Secondary Schools into Learning Schools

*Professional Learning Communities*

Bernice Y Sanchez, PhD

ISBN 978-1-7337412-4-8

# Acknowledgments

Thank you to my family, friends, and mentors who have encouraged me, inspired me, and supported me throughout this process. Writing is a journey of critical thought, reflection, and isolation. Heartfelt thank you and much appreciation, to the school district, educators, and administrators who allowed our team of consultants to become part of your school learning communities. Our team was extremely honored to have worked with amazing teachers who are truly dedicated and committed to student learning. Finally, thank you to family members who are no longer with me on this writing journey on earth, but who are my guardian angels in heaven, thank you for encouraging me to write, when I could not write anymore.

# Table of Contents

# Introduction

Growing up in a southern bilingual border town, family, community and culture united everyone together. Traditions and cultural values drove the everyday functionality of the small border town. As a young child and student growing up in a bilingual community, my fondest memories of teachers in the early grades were those that were comforting, nurturing, and inspiring to be your best self. Some teachers I was able to relate to and connect with, while others I felt a sense of disconnect. I was fortunate to have some really remarkable teachers and mentors over the years that provided me the foundation and in-depth connections to truly appreciate literature, science, and history. Some of my teachers had a unique ability to bring learning to life in the classroom communities that I was fortunate to be part of. I had memorable elementary and secondary level teachers that encouraged me and instilled lifelong learning skills. I also had teachers whose behaviors indicated that teaching may not have been their first professional career choice. All in all, I am grateful to all the teachers and mentors that contributed to the evolution of my career path (the positive and the negative experiences). Every teacher I have encountered has shaped and molded me into the educator that I am today. The teachers I distinctly remember are those that always left me feeling valued, accepted, inspired, and with a sense of belonging to a classroom community. As Maya Angelou states so eloquently, "I've learned that people will forget what you said, people will forget what you did, but people will never forget how you made them feel."

When I left my hometown community to attend university, I encountered similar experiences in my undergraduate and graduate studies with university communities of support and encouragement. My best memories are those from my experiences at Texas Woman's University.

Being away from the southern border and emerged into diverse cultural communities of students from all over the world allowed me to experience university life in a community of deeper and higher learning that I had never experienced before. The professors become mentors and part of my extended family. The communities of friendships are still part of my life today. The dynamics of that university community culture provided a foundation for the endless possibilities that were ahead. The university community memorandum was that all students were capable of anything they set their mind to, anything is possible and that we are the determiners of our future and we are responsible for setting our own boundaries and limits. I was fortunate to be part of university communities of professors who were supportive and were determined that all students could do great things.

As a child growing up in the seventies, I have affectionate memories of forming strong friendship communities with my school peers and neighborhood children in my community. Strong bonds grew out of those communities formed many years ago, and they still exist today. As I reflect on growing up in a southern border town and on my diverse college life experiences, I often revert to that idea of "community" and how communities can lift you up, inspire you and carry you through life's challenges. At the same time, individuals within the communities could also bring you down and challenge your own capabilities and beliefs, including your faith and place on this earth. Strong communities (family, school friends, teachers, mentors and neighbors) that encompass trust, commitment, and faith in each other were always those that seem to exist and transcend time; those were the communities I was always drawn to. The very idea that it takes a village, a community, or family to raise a child has always influenced and guided my thinking process over the years in terms of how to best develop lifelong learning students. My experiences with communities growing up always inspired me to look ahead to how I could replicate these nurturing communities that contributed to my upbringing and to my journey of lifelong learning. I often reflect on, how an individual is raised in an environment with a pathway influenced by external factors beyond one's control, but only the individual self can make life choices to stay on that course or to deviate from the path. It is that pathway that is influenced by the various communities one chooses to participate in throughout life.

Communities by definition are a social unit of small groups with similar interests or characteristics that are drawn together socially or by community conformity. Communities share common interests, place of organization, and similar practices. Some communities are formed for purposes of organizing for a certain cause or forge together to ascertain certain goals as the primary purpose. Other communities are formed based on friendships, locality, or in times of crisis. Regardless, communities are units of individuals that bond together and are built on trust and develop over time.

AP ?

A learning experience that further explored my inquiry on the power of communities occurred when I embarked on my first teaching job as a middle school English/Language Arts teacher in the suburbs of Dallas. I found myself engaged with the many challenges often encountered by first-year teachers. I had acquired extensive knowledge of application of pedagogical approaches through my student teaching experiences and I had great enthusiasm and excitement about teaching middle school. My biggest challenge, at the onset, was discipline and effective classroom management skills. Discipline and classroom management for adolescents were key to providing an environment where classroom instruction could thrive. I spent months trying to improve on the discipline component to teaching and had some success, but this took several months into the year. The suburb I was teaching in was predominately Hispanic and African- American students, in a low-income community. About 90% of my students lived in housing project communities, and the neighborhoods were infested with drugs and gang violence. Drive-by shootings and police presence was the norm in this community. The odds of these adolescents succeeding in life were slim and the expectations were low. The home community environments where students resided influenced how they viewed education on the spectrum of importance within their lives; their community lives focused on day-to-day survival. Food on the table and roof over their heads were the daily challenges that my students encountered. Advancing ones' education was not highly valued in these communities, which made it challenging to discipline students.

Finally, when I had reached some level of classroom management, middle school students were not interested in the instructional delivery of materials, writing prompts or topics I provided for writing instruction. After attempting different pedagogical modes and a variety of delivery methods, I keep asking where I had gone wrong; I felt that I had failed my students because nothing seemed to get through to them. My coworkers often complimented me on the great work for a first-year teacher, for I had eventually developed good classroom management skills, and everyone was civil with no major incidents. Somehow, I was not convinced that this was the best that I could offer my students. I keep trying to understand my students' sense of community, but I had not grown up in the same community environment. My students came from challenged home environments. Some of my students resided in the projects in South East Dallas; others were homeless, and some had been abandoned by their parents and were living with grandparents, or other extended family members or in foster care. I expected students to come to school ready and motivated to learn, when on the contrary they were struggling with basic needs. I often worried for my students as they would share stories of harassment by gang members on the walk home from school daily. I understood that as teachers we, the community of teachers, could not solve or

4

change their home community environments; however, I was determined from a problem solver perspective that we could do something in the classroom to begin to shed light on the importance and potential outcomes of advancing their education by building positive communities of teachers and communities of students.

Near the end of spring semester of my first-year teaching, a previous past tragic event got me to thinking more deeply about students' community and what mattered most to them. The entire middle school community was in mourning and in remembrance of the death of a famous Latina singer on the one-year anniversary. This day was a teaching moment opportunity about how I viewed my students and what they valued in their communities. I distinctly remember students crying in the school halls and in my English class. Students' behavior was different that day, difficult to describe, not the traditional day-to-day tough persona. In my mind, the lesson plan for the day had been discarded, and now plan B had just evolved. I communicated to my students that because of the events of this one-year anniversary in their community, now my community, we would discuss why this famous singer was so important to them and their family and in their communities. Their responses surprised me; these adolescents actually cared deeply about this individual. Students communicated how she had advanced the level of their community and how she had made the Latin community proud; they had someone to look up to, a role model. This was a teaching moment, and for the first time, I saw my adolescent students not as students, but as compassionate human beings that actually had a sense of community belonging and cared about those that represented their community. I asked my students to write on a piece of paper how they felt about the singer, how connected they were to her, and how she was representative of their community. I asked them to discuss their grief and sense of loss into written words. This, of course, was a disguise for an essay assignment; but I failed to mention that, I just asked them to write.

Surprisingly, or maybe not, I received elaborate drafts of potentially well-organized thoughts and ideas. I finally got students to write on a topic that mattered to them and their essays certainly had voice in them, but more importantly I felt as if I had tapped into their communities. The essays were riddled with grammatical errors and as Peter Elbow would say "bad, writing," but this is the best form of writing that establishes the foundation for good writing. This did not matter as students had voice and had messages they wanted to communicate, and this was the perfect venue for it. I felt their loss and grief, and I was now part of their community through their writing. The anniversary of her tragic death brought a sense of awareness of how fragile life can be, for these students' daily struggles they could relate. After this teachable moment, I believe that students began to see me as a human being, as someone who had compassion for her students and was attempting to understand their learning styles and needs. It is difficult to explain the dynamics of that first-year teaching and specifically that day. I had to stop being too theoretical and too focused on classroom management and had to work harder at trying to understand my students' home communities. This was the beginning of a process, looking at it from a different perspective, into understanding my students' home environment communities. Within this process of meaningful engagement, I began to transform our learning communities of teacher meetings from just curricular meetings to student assessment profile meetings to best assist and know our students. Our curricular meetings were important to share instructional practices and student performance assessment data, but somehow they needed more of a student development focus. Those conversations were important for the development of our students and how to best meet their needs. This was what I deemed as "Professional Learning Communities," or the early structure of what later came to be known as PLCs. From that point moving forward, my students were all part of a learning community of writers. Things weren't always perfect moving forward, and there were still bumps along the way as I completed my first year of teaching. In any case, it was that sense of community that I reverted back to when I was growing up in a southern border town. Community mattered when it came to students' learning, and so did teacher communities as well. Often times as teachers we see ourselves disconnected from our students and our students' home communities, but a shift in seeing ourselves separate from the world to connected to communities within our students' world, can have transformative results. Reflecting on past and present experiences it is evident, learning is both personal and social, and it connects us to each other (Senge, Cambron-McCabe, Lucas, Smith, Dutton, & Kleiner, 2012).

The following book seeks to provide educators, school administrators, and researchers, with an overview of theories and research on teacher development and a narrative discourse of the impact of Professional Learning Communities in action in secondary schools in South Texas. In addition, the book provides opportunities to engage in dialog, critical reflection, and ideas for engaging in reflective action.

Chapter 1 describes the school systems across the country and the challenges encountered due to accountability and school reform. A discussion on transformational schools in theory is provided and the chapter concludes with questions for reflection and further engagement on the power of transformation.

Chapter 2 provides an overview of past traditional staff development in comparison to current professional development trends. An overview of teacher support including mentoring, modeling, and coaching are provided. Extended discussion and research provided on professional learning communities and challenges encountered during implementation. Chapter 2 concludes with questions for reflection and further engagement regarding teacher support.

Chapter 3 describes the three-year grant initiative model and the foundation for its inception at the designated middle school campuses. The following chapter provides educator and administrator narrative accounts of their experiences with professional learning communities in action at their respective campus. The chapter concludes with questions for further reflective dialog and action regarding learning communities.

Chapter 4 provides teacher survey respondent results on specific teacher support services and an overview of the lessons learned from the professional communities in action. Chapter 4 concludes with questions for reflection and further engagement through action.

The conclusion provides an overall reflection of lessons learned from the impact of communities to how communities of educators can transform into learning schools.

## Questions for Reflection

1) What are your early memories of communities you participated in the past?
2) Identify characteristics of current communities you participate in.
3) Describe those communities that you feel have impacted your life.
4) Describe a past experience of an educator who left a lasting impression on you as a student. Positive/Negative.
5) Describe an occurrence where you as a classroom teacher had a teachable moment with your students.

## Responses:

# Chapter I: Transformational Schools in Theory

School systems across the country have been on the decline for decades and the infusion of Common Core Standards has elevated the expectations and accountability for school districts across the US. Now, more than ever, school systems are searching for ways to improve student academic performance, teacher instruction, and overall school improvement efforts for constructive school environments. Accountability has contributed to the educational landscape for the past five decades. The focus on accountability since the 1990s has concentrated on issues of adequacy. The *No Child Left Behind Act (NCLB)* was enacted to increase academic achievement for all students and improve educational institutions. Accountability has been prevalent throughout the years and administrators and educators continue to be unsuccessful at meeting the academic standards set by the state and federal accountability structures hence the decline across the US (Styron & Styron, 2011).

Administrators, curriculum leaders, and teachers are challenged to figure out ways to develop creative approaches to developing effective leaders and creating effective learning environments. Teacher support services for novice and veteran teachers and collaboration among teachers and administration at all levels can have a significant impact. The importance of teacher support for purposes of teacher retention and effective classroom instruction and student improvement overall are critical. According to Scherer's (2012) conversation with Darling-Hammond, teachers who have engaged in student teaching programs and are knowledgeable in preparation elements of classroom practice including child development studies are less likely to leave the profession after the first year. Furthermore, student teacher candidates who have observed other teachers, been observed themselves and offered feedback, and coached throughout the process are less than half as likely to leave within the first year. National standards signify that 20-30% of novice teachers leave the profession within the first five years, and the attrition is higher (50%) or more in high-poverty designated schools and this includes high need subject areas including Math and Sciences (Guha, Hyler, & Darling-Hammond, 2017). Novice teachers and experienced teachers want to be in successful classroom environments where they are supported by colleagues, curriculum specialists, and principals within the profession in collaborative community environments. Schools that foster and build these classrooms and school environments provide teachers opportunities to grow and refine their teaching. According to Scherer's (2012) conversation with Darling-Hammond, for these environments to thrive, school schedules and systems must be reorganized. School administrators need to personalize and structure support and professional development that seems outside of the norm, if these environments are what provides teacher support and enhance instruction, then all these must work in sync with each other to engineer success.

Strauss (2013) quotes Darling-Hammond in *The Washington Post,* "Achieving reform related goals in public schools will require a transformation in teaching, learning, and assessment so that all students develop the deeper learning competencies that are necessary for post secondary success" (para. 3). Furthermore, reform that focuses on construction of new learning standards and assessments are effective only if all involved in the process work together (administration, stakeholders, district leaders, and teachers). Unfortunately, instruction that is top down curriculum prescriptive by reformers can impede learning and impact teacher development. Development of expertise on enhancing literacy skills including reading, writing, listening, thinking critically, communicating effectively (oral and written), and reflection are needed. According to Strauss

(2013), teachers need opportunities to work in collaboration with peers with purposeful action in efforts to deepen their literacy learning and improve their teaching and learning practices. Teachers need time to improve their teaching practices and to collaborate with peers in order for change and transformation in teaching, learning, and assessment to develop.

Darling-Hammond, Wei, Andree, Richardson, Orphanos (2009) conducted a study entitled *"Professional learning in the learning profession: A status report on teacher development in the United States and abroad"* published by the National Staff Development Council. They used data surveys collected from 1999-2008 and measured a variety of factors including specifically teachers' perceptions regarding their professional development experiences and opportunities. The overall findings in this report indicated that the professional development available for educators across 50 states focused on educators' academic content knowledge, showcased growing attention to mentoring coaching support, and targeted new teachers. However, overall, the high-intensity, job-embedded collaborative deep learning that is most effective was not a common feature of professional development across most states, districts, and schools in the United States.

> *Professional development is most effective when it addresses the concrete, everyday challenges involved in teaching and learning specific academic subject matter....When schools are strategic in creating time and productive working relationships within academic departments or grade levels, across them, or among teachers school wide, the benefits can include better instruction and more success in solving problems of practice.* (Darling-Hammond et al., 2009, p. 10-11)

## Transformational Theories

Transformational theory is a theoretical framework or foundation for how to move progressively through a process that requires reflection and the ability to suspend preconceptions and embrace the challenges and the power to change. Transformation can be positive, or negative,

13

with a positive approach in mind it must be goal orientated with guidance and support. Transformation requires a new approach, a new way of being, and a new set of tools, and different lenses from which to view the current state. Transformation, in the context of school systems, is an on-going, collaborative process which can sometimes be met with resistance to change.

Transformational teaching emphasizes critical thinking and communication skills where opportunities for students to apply new skills and perspectives are the focus. According to Aguilar (2013), transformational coaching involves three domains which include the interconnectiveness of 1) teachers' beliefs, behaviors, and being 2) institution and systems of people within 3) broader educational and social systems one resides in. While everyone agrees that public school systems require reform and attention to issues impacting our educational systems, authentic transformational teaching and coaching are components of the transformation process.

Mezirow's (2000) theory of transformational learning is an adult learning theory that combines positive development and learning. Mezirow's (1991) transformative learning theory utilizes issues or dilemmas to challenge one's own thinking. The theory is a developmental process where the learner understands that the process of using prior knowledge and interpretations construct a new or updated version of meaning of one's own experiences in order to guide future action. Mezirow (1991) has differentiated among three types of reflection that include content reflection, process reflection, and premise reflection. While all are fundamental, premise reflection or critical reflection on experience where one examines values, beliefs, and socially constructed assumptions are the key to transformational learning. Experience, critical reflection, and rational discourse are the processes where transformative learning occurs. Learning that transforms challenging frames of reference to make them more inclusive, reflective, dialogic, and emotionally able to change is the framework for the *Professional Learning Communities* suggested here

14

(Mezirow, 1991). *Professional learning* is situated within the transformative learning theoretical framework.

Murray and Sheninger (2017) suggest that transforming teacher learning in America should be a priority in the US. They suggest this generation of school children need to be better prepared and require knowledge of more complex material in order to be successful in the next century. Murray and Sheninger (2017) agree with Stanford professor and researcher Darling-Hammond that professional development opportunities have not been successful in US schools in providing teachers' opportunities and support to improve their craft. Professional development in some high-achieving nations include the following characteristics not often found in US Schools: 1) teacher learning opportunities over time 2) teacher professional learning built into teacher work hours 3) teacher learning opportunities involving active learning and collaboration 4) professional development focused on specific content areas to be taught 5) teachers involved in the decisions regarding curriculum, assessment, and professional development. In addition, what are lacking in US schools are opportunities for reflection and collegial discussions worked into teachers' daily work schedules with ongoing continued support. According to Murray and Sheninger (2017), the concept of one day or two day workshops with no follow up, do not lead to productivity or effective reflection or instruction. US schools lack the structures and support to sustain collaborative teacher professional learning that leads to real improvements.

Once in the classroom environment, educators transition into scholar-practitioner leaders within the context of transformational theory, and that is when true change happens when scholarship informs practice and practice influences scholarship. Educators must be informed on what the scholarship or research suggests for their area of instruction, and this can be accomplished through collaboration among teacher peers and building teacher communities. That scholarship and knowledge of students within their classrooms is what informs their practice and their instruction and delivery of instructional approaches. Practitioner indicates one who practices and understands the importance of knowledge-based content in collaboration with the research for effective leadership (Hampton, 2010).

Scholar–practitioner leaders require a growth mindset approach to classroom learning and practice. As teachers we must understand that teaching is a practice and a process and not perfection. This then becomes the teacher's beliefs that are then transferred and encouraged onto students who engage in the approach that learning is a process and a journey towards one that entails mistakes alongside discovery. Brock and Hundley (2016) describe the growth mind-set approach as taking on challenges with the belief that perseverance, effort, and practice can have limitless potential to grow and learn; this applies to both teacher and student, and are all consistent within the transformational approach in theory.

Transformational teaching, transformational coaching, transformational learning are all extensions of transformational theory in the general sense. When transformational theory is applied, schools evolve and develop out of these principles and establish the foundation for school change and reform.

## Questions for Reflection

1) Describe the dynamics of your current school system.
2) What are the challenges encountered by your district and campus regarding state accountability?
3) Describe professional development at your campus/district.
4) Describe your thoughts on transformation (teaching, coaching, and learning). How do you envision your school campus in the context of the transformation process?

## Responses:

# Chapter II: Teacher Support

Teaching is a craft that requires practice, attention to detail, and fine tuning. Teaching is an on-going practice and process-oriented journey that requires a growth mindset. There are no mistakes in the practice of teaching as everything that happens within teachers' daily teaching practice is an opportunity to improve on this craft.

Teaching, within the belief that it is a craft, is aligned to the transformational theory of transforming public school systems. Transformation of schools requires a transformation in teaching, learning, and assessment within a collaborative critical reflective community environment. Teacher support is important to transforming schools and this can take on various forms including mentoring, modeling, coaching, professional development, and professional learning communities. The types of teacher support and professional development has transformed as educational institutions have evolved. Historically, Kragler, Martin, and Sylvester (2014) have acknowledged stages of transition of educators' professional development learning and how it has evolved over the last several decades. These include: in-service period 1950's-1960's, staff development period 1970's-1980's, professional development period 1990-2000, and professional learning period mid-2000 to the present. This current era for professional learning is about creating professional learning communities that encourage collaborative and critical reflective learning and engagement. This period is about multiple opportunities for engagement within teachers' own thinking and informed decision making that advances teachers' knowledge and expertise. The very core of learning communities consists of inquiry, reflective dialogue, and mutual respect and collaboration amongst school educators and administrators. The following chart provides a reflective overview of the transformation of teacher support from what was characteristic of staff

and professional development opposed to current trends in professional learning communities.

# Traditional Staff and Professional Development vs. Professional Learning Communities

| Traditional Staff and Professional Development | Professional Learning Communities |
|---|---|
| Campus administration are leaders and make decisions regarding instruction and assessment | Administration and teachers are collaborative participants in the decision making process regarding instruction and assessment |
| Teachers are provided in-service workshops, passive receivers of knowledge, and have little to no input in the process | Staff and administration collaborate on teaching and learning needs for small group meetings or mini-workshops and all participants are active and reflective practitioners of knowledge |
| Goals are short term and quantified increases in student performance through immediate results of data collection | Goals are long term and flexible. Student performance is measured over time and sustainable through multiple modes of assessment (informal & formal). Measurement includes quantified and qualitative means of data collection |
| Administration and teachers isolated and little to no follow through regarding workshops | Administration and teachers work in collaboration and with continuity through regular small group meeting sessions with follow up sessions including action groups and peer coaching based on student needs |
| Training mindset designed for teachers and instructed what to teach and how to teach | Collaboration amongst all stakeholders and teachers are encouraged to engage in inquiry and reflective practices on instructional design and delivery |

# Mentoring, Modeling, and Coaching

A mentor is often described as one who provides guidance, direction, and support as a means of encouraging and providing initial support within various realms of learning. A mentor-teacher in education can be a cooperating teacher (assigned within student teaching program), a veteran campus teacher to assist a first-year teacher; or a consultant or campus specialist can also serve in the capacity of a mentor to support the development of both novice and experienced teachers. Mentors can take on the role of supporting teachers by supporting them through professional development and guidance of instructional practices and effective classroom strategies. Mentors can also serve as positive role models for teachers in their early teaching experiences by providing emotional supportive and non-evaluative support within their academic community environments. Numerous studies by Odell and Ferraro (1992) and Chapman (1983) primarily on first-year teachers has suggested that teachers who were provided both instructional and emotional mentoring support to beginning teachers may have a valuable impact on teacher retention and teacher confidence in the classroom.

A study conducted by Koleman, Roegman, Goodwin (2017) examined the mentoring practices of a group of strong mentor-teachers. The study refers to the term "learner-centered mentoring" as a means of understanding the learner within a developmental trajectory, in this being the candidate undergoing the mentorship. Within this context, learner-centered mentoring begins with the knowledge and skills the teacher-candidate brings to the classroom and learning occurs through experiences provided in the classroom environment made available by the mentor teacher. This study along with others (Boreen, Johson, Niday, & Potts, 2000) has concluded that good mentor-teachers are both reflective and understand that mentoring is a relational process where the mentor provides a warm environment inclusive of emotional support. Other characteristics of good mentor teachers cited in these studies is the mentoring of teacher candidates should be less generic and unscripted and instead more responsive to teacher candidates unique learning needs. This includes a focus on mentoring conversations around problems of practice. Discussions on how experienced teachers make mistakes and that practice in inquiry and reflection are part of the on-going teaching process/journey. This gradual release of responsibility process was a unique characteristic displayed by good mentor-teachers. Koleman, Roegman, Goodwin (2017) suggest that the growth mind set as described by Dweck (2008) is aligned with the characteristics of good-mentor teachers who encourage risks and reflection of understanding candidates' readiness and learning needs.

Modeling takes on different forms and is a characteristic of effective mentor-teachers. While modeling teaching practices are important for candidates' growth, it should not be the only form of modeling projected to candidates. In a learner-centered approach, modeling is a means of teaching how to teach based on the candidate's readiness and is a contrast to more traditional replication of practices. In a learner-centered mentoring approach, the process begins with identifying the unique and individual learning needs of candidates through a constant cycle of gradual release involving reflection, experimentation, learning from mistakes, and professional development.

Bandura's Social Learning Theory posits that people learn from one another, via observation, imitation, and modeling. People learn through observing others' behavior, attitudes, and outcomes of those behaviors. "Most human behavior is learned observationally through modeling: from observing others, one forms an idea of how new behaviors are performed, and on later occasions this coded information serves as a guide for action" (Bandura, 1977, p. 22).

Kelly Gallagher (2011) suggested that over the years of teaching writing and in writing conversations with teachers the best form of teaching writing is through modeling. Modeling for students is one of the most effective instructional approaches according to Gallagher. It is important that teachers be comfortable with modeling for their students and engage in the practice regularly regardless of the subject content matter. If teachers are expected to model for students, it is important that teachers are both knowledgeable and comfortable with the content. Research informs us that modeling can be an effective instructional strategy for teaching students, but it is important that teachers have the skill set, preparedness, and support to be able to model for students.

Diez (2007) describes the importance of modeling for teacher candidates as a way of preparing them to serve as effective models themselves. Diez (2007) noted, "When teacher educators take on the responsibility to both conceptualize the abilities required for effective teaching and to model those for their teacher candidates, they are beginning the process for transforming teacher education from a collection of courses to a developmental process" (p.394). Thus, modeling for teacher candidates is one component of transforming schools.

Mentoring and modeling all play vital roles in the transformation of teachers and school environments. Coaching is another component in this transformation process, and this approach also takes on various forms. For example, directive coaching is focused on changing teachers' behaviors and practices where the coach is seen as an expert in the field who is tasked with teaching a set of skills to teacher candidates. Another form of coaching within this model is known as facilitative coaching where the Zone of Proximal Development is the focus. The coach supports the teacher in learning new ways of thinking and being reflective, through analysis, through observation, and experimental practices, and this awareness influences their behavior. The coach in this model does not necessarily share expert content knowledge, but builds on the teacher's existing skills to help the teacher construct new knowledge that will form the basis for future actions. Transformational coaching is a combination of strategies from directive and facilitative and is directed at and affects all 3 domains. This includes teacher behaviors, beliefs and being, institutional systems department teams and students, and broader educational and social systems we live in. Transformational coaching is not something that is done to another, but rather it is a dynamic engagement between coach and candidate who work together to establish a relational journey oriented by goals created collaboratively through a system thinking approach (Aguilar, 2013). Coaching is one of the best forms contributing to professional development that can bring out potential in people and uncover their strengths and skills while building emotionally resilient educators. Apprenticeship, while viewed as an antiquated form of coaching, is similar where an experienced practitioner encourages and supports the learner in the learning trajectory realm where they are (positioned). Coaching is a fundamental component of any effective professional development program. It has the ability to build on knowledge and skills, to tap into practices and feelings of the educator, and establish conditions where learning and reflection can develop. These conditions create an environment where conversations about risks and failures are all part of the growth process. These are all characteristics that make coaching so invaluable in all classroom settings (Aguilar, 2013)

There is a wide range of research in the area of coaching. A comprehensive study by the *Annenberg Institute for School Reform* on Instructional Coaching was conducted in 2004. The elements of instructional coaching provide a framework for research on professional learning communities and professional development. Overall, the report concluded various important findings based on the idea that coaching is in part an element of a professional development program. First, it concluded that effective coaching encourages reflective and collaborative practices which are a shift and move any from direct instruction environments. The second finding is that effective embedded professional development in conjunction with coaching promotes positive cultural changes within the school environment that moves beyond just impacting content instruction. Next, coaching alongside professional development was linked to teachers' increase in using data to inform practice as a form of using the data to target and address specific areas of need. Finally, effective coaching distributes leadership among the stakeholders, and it helps in maintaining the focus on teaching and learning through reciprocal accountability (Annenberg Institute for School Reform, 2004).

Joyce and Showers (2002) extensive research on the concept of coaching has contributed to the shift from traditional staff development to the current professional learning communities. Joyce and Showers (2002) contend that "learning how to learn" is equally significant as teacher professional development and acquisition of new knowledge and skills. They describe a model of coaching in which collaborative planning and resource development including peer observations and learning from each other are critical in the learning how to learn model. Joyce and Showers (2002) have documented significant increases in student achievement and learning when both teachers and administrators were engaged in ongoing support in combination with quality professional development that included inquiry practice and modeling. The key element was that knowledge gained by teachers had to be transferred into classroom practice in order to be impactful on student learning.

Overall, the research suggests that coaching can build relationships amongst school systems and when embedded in a system supported campus and district wide which addresses teacher and student needs alongside shared responsibility and accountability can improve teaching and learning and provide the platform for school reform and transformation (Annenberg Institute for School Reform, 2004; Joyce, & Showers, 1985; Joyce and Showers, 2002; Aguilar, 2013).

## Professional Learning Communities

Teacher support in the form of mentoring, modeling, and coaching all play a significant role in transforming teaching and learning. According to Darling-Hammond and Richardson (2009), professional learning communities, this new decade of professional development, provide a structure for all these elements in what matters in teacher learning. Lent (2007) describes professional learning communities as living and breathing processes constantly evolving and vary from school to school. The fluidity of professional learning communities in education is reflective of any form of community, with unique characteristics, one participates in. She asserts that effective professional learning communities should stem from the needs of the community and should focus on exploration rather than just current trends in teaching and learning. According to Lent (2007), current research has provided a new paradigm for professional development that is contrary to the one-day and lack of follow up of the antiquated workshop models. Current models of high-quality professional development include a variety of factors and involve multiple stakeholders in the process. This includes teacher's content knowledge and how students learn specific content. Opportunities for teachers to acquire new knowledge inclusive of practice and reflection that is aligned with curriculum, standards, and assessment are part of this model. This involves administrative support and sustained collaboration over time for these learning communities to be successful and effective (Darling-Hammond & Richardson, 2009).

Lee, Smith, and Croninger (1995) conducted a study of 820 secondary schools across the country and concluded that in schools that were identified as learning communities all stakeholders engaged in collective responsibility for the learning of students and consistently worked in

27

collaboration with each other and adjusted their teaching for the advancement of their students learning. The end result of these schools was that students had higher academic performance in the areas of science, history, math and literacy than those in conventional professional development organized school model. Additionally, according to the researchers, teachers in these learning communities school model also reported fewer absentees and appeared more optimistic and satisfied with their work environments.

Margalef and Roblin (2016) describe professional learning communities as a center for improving student learning through collaborative and aligned professional development within the school environment of teachers' own challenges and practice. They conducted a study on the roles of facilitators in professional learning communities in higher education. Margalef and Roblin (2016) conducted multiple case studies and documented their responses. Their findings revealed that the roles of the facilitators were constantly changing and evolving to adapt to the needs of the community and the participating entities. Learning communities are constantly evolving, and those facilitating these learning communities must adapt and depend on continuous feedback in the process to be effective. As Margalef and Roblin (2016) researched the roles of facilitators within professional learning communities they also collectively cited various studies that indicated that educator collaboration within the schools can have significant positive effects on both teaching and learning (Lomos, Hofman, & Bosker, 2011; Dogan, Pringle, & Mesa, 2015; Vescio, Ross, & Adams, 2008).

Lumpe (2007) and Senge (2006) suggest that learning communities play a vital role in general for all learning organizations and are also applicable to the field of education. Lumpe (2007) contends that meaningful collaboration is the focus of professional learning communities and teachers are often isolated within the current school structure systems. Professional learning communities in education include peer coaching and teacher leadership structures designed to foster true and meaningful collaboration focused on meaningful topics and student learning. Professional learning communities, as described by Lumpe (2007), are structured around development that includes curriculum and instruction and assessment and involves practice, reflection, and collaboration within distributed leadership school communities and this is reflective of the cooperate world.

Senge (2006) also describes learning organizations as an art and the practice of five disciplines that are easily applicable to educational systems. Senge' learning organization representation is reflective of professional learning community models. The five disciplines include: personal mastery, mental models, building a shared vision, team learning, and systems thinking. Senge (2006) asserts that personal mastery is the ability of continuously improving one's craftsmanship or level of proficiency with a focus on becoming a lifelong learner. This coincides with my rooted beliefs, mentioned previously; teaching is a craft that is a process-oriented journey and requires a growth mind set. Senge (2006) describes mental models as assumptions or mental images that impact how we interpret messages and how we perceive the outside world. These mental models affect our external behavior, so it is important to understand deeply the accuracy of those mental models. The next discipline outlined by Senge (2006) is building a shared vision which requires genuine vision inclusive of all participants with a common destiny. To dictate a vision and provide vision statements is the contrary to this discipline. Team learning, according to Senge (2006), is the ability to take that shared vision and develop it into authentic team learning where dialogue and participants are reflecting together and collaborating together. Teams must be able to learn together and identify patterns of interaction and engagement as a way of moving forward. A combination of these characteristics of these disciplines reflects Mezirow's (2000) theory of transformational learning where learning transforms challenging frames of reference to make them more inclusive, reflective, dialogic, and emotionally and mentally able to change.

The fifth and final discipline, systems thinking, according to Senge (2006), brings all the other disciplines together. This is the understanding that organizations function more effectively when they are viewed as whole organizations and not individual parts. Practicing all the disciplines concurrently allows us to see how we think, how we interact, and how we learn. Through Senge's systems thinking approach, we begin to understand how we are connected to the learning organization, understand and see problems from varying perspectives, and how our actions create our own experiences. This art and practice is reminiscent of my experiences my first year teaching. As highlighted in the introduction, often times as teachers we see ourselves disconnected from our students and our students' home communities, but a shift in seeing ourselves separate from the world to connected to communities within our students' world, can have transformative results. Professional learning characteristics are consistent with this practice of learning organizations in that reflective dialogue, looking within, and everyone working collaboratively with a shared vision is constant.

Dennis Sparks (2002) wrote a book entitled *Designing Powerful Professional Development for Teachers and Principals* and the message resonates with today's current trends in professional development. Sparks' (2002) message is that communities of practice are "learning communities." The book is focused on the premise that professional development has not proved to be effective and extensive research has documented this; however, the actual practice of professional development for the most part remains static. Sparks (2002) established the foundation and groundwork for professional learning communities in his book by elaborating on the elements of powerful professional development practiced and sustained learning through collegial learning, inquiry approach, and experimentation through continuity as part of daily practice. In addition to, small group meetings of teachers consistently on a regular basis and expanding teachers' content knowledge with a deep learning focus approach that requires reflection and dialogue are critical. Sparks (2002) contends that dialogue amongst all educators and administrators in a supportive environment of empathy with suspension of judgments are crucial. Internal reflection of assumptions and stereotypes are critical towards deeper understanding and learning towards building common bonds and bridges towards a shared vision of goals. A supportive school culture of encouragement and motivation and mutual respect from all educators and administrators is the heart of all progressively functioning professional learning schools. According to Sparks (2002) creating schools where everyone, involved in the process, has a job to learn and develop as a practitioner, then and only then can powerful professional learning occur.

Risko and Vogt (2016) use the term professional learning instead of professional development as a means to describe a shift in stages for educators' learning moving away from the traditional modes. Professional learning trajectory begins when educators transition from moving away from being told what to do as educators towards a trajectory moving towards directing their own learning and problem-solving agendas. Risko and Vogt (2016) claim that this view of educators taking responsibility for their own professional learning through problem solving or inquiry is framed within the social constructivist view and Mezirow's (2000) theory of transformational learning. Risko and Vogt (2016) developed a synergistic framework of Professional Learning as an Inquiry Process. They focused on *problem solving, learning and doing,* and *responding and transforming* (p.15). Risko and Vogt (2016) assert that professional learning begins with teachers actively engaged in *problem solving* authentic problems within their classrooms and campuses and reflecting on what are the factors contributing to these problems including needs assessment. Next, *learning and doing* in this inquiry process involves establishing goals and reflecting and honoring multiple perspectives. According to Risko and Vogt (2016), professional learning must be "substantive" in that acquisition of knowledge must be established and practiced at a deeper level. In addition, proposing solutions to teaching and monitoring learning and reflecting on feedback which involves ongoing dialogue are crucial to this process. Finally, Risko and Vogt (2016) bring all elements together by responding and transforming within this inquiry process by examination of the changes and adapting changes with goals as needed. In this case, responding to problems and needs while aligning student performance with standards. This includes transforming teaching practices and supporting students' literacy achievement. All in all, they suggest that professional learning is *personal*. The power behind professional learning is that it must be differentiated support to meet individual needs for each campus and district is what accounts for effective and authentic professional learning.

## Challenges Transitioning into Learning Communities

While the characteristics and positive effects of learning communities have been well documented, educational systems across the country seem to hesitate and fail to embrace fully the necessary components of authentic professional learning communities. One challenge, mentioned earlier in this chapter, is the "accountability shuffle" and lack of measurable proof or sustainable time to allow change to take place as argued by Lent (2007). The practice of professional learning communities is not easily measured with immediate data as they are evolving entities that vary by campus and district and measurability occurs over time. Transformational and sustainable change occurs over time, but with the pressure of state accountability standards and immediate data results showcasing measurable student performance; this contradicts progressive change. School districts often find themselves siding with accountability constraints aligned with standardized testing rather than opportunities for collaboration and deep learning and reflection. Another challenge is the lack of trust among educators and administrators including poor quality relationships that exist in many schools. In addition, school systems challenged by poverty and other social issues can also impact how and to what extent learning communities are incorporated into schools.

According to Meier's (2002) *In Schools We Trust*, public schools are failing to meet the academic needs of students and will continue to do so until educational reform shifts away from standardized testing and approaches organizing our school systems within a culture of trust, collaboration, and community building. Meier (2002) stresses the importance of students' learning alongside educators within a continuum of teaching and learning. She goes further by encouraging parental involvement and the importance of educators to become involved in their students' communities and develop awareness of students' cultural differences. Furthermore, Meier (2002) makes a strong argument that standardized testing provides a superficial measure of accountability and academic competence and is counterproductive to student learning.

In *A Fifth Discipline: Schools that Learn* Senge et al. (2012) assert that all communities should be invested in this connection between living and learning and long-term community wide cultures of learning. Relationships, observations, and teacher experiences must develop in communities of trust where they are not measurable, but rather ethically valued in that they are significant contributors to student learning. Relationships that are built on trust, collaboration, and dialogue and with student learning as the focus are the driving forces behind learning communities.

Consequently, it is vital that leaders of learning communities make the foundation of high quality relationships and trust a high priority and move beyond the standardized accountability emphasis with the idea that schools that learn are those in which students and teachers learn and work together in communities of practice, or what is known as learning communities.

## Questions for Reflection

1) As an educator, school leader, or administrator at your campus what is your perception of "*teaching*" in general?
2) What experiences have you engaged in regarding traditional staff and professional development and/or your own professional learning history?
3) What are your past experiences with mentoring, modeling and coaching? What type of teacher support has been the most impactful from your experiences?
4) Describe the current state of teacher support/professional learning communities at your specific campus? What are some of the challenges you foresee in implementing professional learning communities at your school campus?

## Responses:

# Chapter III: Professional Learning Communities in Action: Educators' Narratives

Professional learning communities in action are inclusive of differentiated professional learning. This is the practice of focusing in on teachers' background knowledge and expertise and experience when planning and coordinating and organizing professional learning communities. According to Senge et al. (2012) teachers must engage in the practice of developing a personal vision alongside an evaluation of the current school reality, which he describes as personal mastery. As part of this process, teachers provide insightful information about their strengths, struggles, and fears regarding their teaching practices and approaches and develop their own learning goals for professional learning communities. Differentiated professional learning, while not common practice, can have many benefits as teacher's career trajectory varies from teacher to teacher. According to Risko and Vogt (2016), teachers' trajectory includes pre-service, apprentice, novice, experienced, and master teachers. Because teachers move along this progressive track at varying levels, with some educators remaining in certain trajectories for many years, it is challenging to provide professional development opportunities for teachers in a specific trajectory level. Hence, the reason that differentiated professional learning can be more effective is because it takes teachers' background knowledge and experiences into consideration when professional learning activities are evolving. Professional learning must be embraced with a common purpose and shared vision and this is another learning discipline that builds on the personal mastery discipline (Senge et al., 2012). Furthermore, Senge et al. (2012) assert that reflective thinking and group dialogue and interaction disciplines are characteristics of schools that learn. Schools that learn are those that are engaged in professional active-reflective learning. Sparks (2002) argues the importance of improving teaching, leadership, and learning for all students through transformational powerful professional learning communities.

## Professional Learning in Action

The following narratives were provided voluntarily by teachers at the middle school level. A three-year state-funded grant was awarded for the purposes of providing teacher support at a designated school district in collaboration with Write for Texas and aligned with the National Writing Project Model. The uniqueness of this grant allowed for master educators to serve as consultants and learning community facilitators at four middle school campuses with the primary goal of supporting teachers from all trajectory levels with different forms and levels of services that varied from mentoring, coaching, modeling, co-teaching, mini-professional development sessions to reflective sessions with small groups of teachers. Professional learning communities' foundations were introduced at different levels for each of the four middle school campuses, each with varying and diverse needs. The primary objective of the grant and overall mission was to provide teacher support at the secondary level to priority-designated district schools, support that would vary based on individual campus and teacher needs; team learning support would be provided in the areas of reading and writing across content areas within the context of critical thinking. The grant support was of no cost to the district with only campus commitment and teacher and administrative participation. Overall, campus administration viewed our resources as an opportunity to improve potentially state testing scores. Campus administration focus was viewed through the accountability framework established by the state of Texas. The primary goal collaboratively was to develop differentiated professional learning communities within each priority designated campus and support teachers in the areas of reading, writing, and critical thinking.

The three-year grant initiative, aligned with the Write for Texas objectives and based on the National Writing Project Model, began with an introduction to district and school administrators. The meetings followed with each individual middle school campus. These meetings involved all Reading/Language Arts educators primarily, and some campuses requested all content area teacher participation. These began as large group settings then transitioned into small group settings. The purpose of these meetings was to have open discussions and reflective dialogue with teachers through informal needs assessment-based conversations in efforts to understand the needs of the campus and the teachers both on a professional and a personal level. The goal of each needs assessment meeting with small groups of teachers at each campus was to understand the structure and functionality of their campus literacy programs and gain a general understanding of the strengths, areas that needed improvement, and daily struggles of the teachers. This was the first step towards building communities of teachers while learning about their institution of learning and starting to understand how it could transition into what Senge et al. (2012) describes as a "learning organization." Once the team of master teachers (consultants) established a campus profile for each of the four middle schools, then the next step or goal was to meet with campus teachers and have them bring campus student data in the areas of Reading and Writing to assess student data collaboratively to understand better student needs (both informal and formal assessment instruments). Some campuses welcomed this process; other campuses had established their own needs assessments and were interested in specific teacher driven professional development that focused on student areas of need. As an external entity we made every effort to honor each specific campus request. The campuses where teachers participated in the brief small group grade level sessions with consultants gave teachers an opportunity to connect both personally and professionally as most teachers commented that they often found themselves disconnected from other teachers on their campus. These responses coincided with and reflected the national research on teachers' disconnection from other teachers:

> As researchers have shown many times over the past three decades, the nation's teachers exhibit a strongly individualistic ethos, owing largely to the built-in privacy and isolation of their daily work as it has been organized in most U.S. schools. Given the prevalence of an "eggcrate model" of instruction—whereby each teacher spends most of the day in a single room, separated from other adults— the American teaching profession has not yet developed a strong tradition of professional collaboration. Historically, schools have been structured so that teachers work alone, rarely given time together to plan lessons, share instructional practices, assess students, design curriculum, or help make administrative or managerial decisions. Such cultural norms are not easily changed, particularly if school structures and working conditions continue to favor privacy and isolation. (Darling-Hammond et al., 2009, p.11)

It was communicated by many of the teachers at these designated campuses that collaboration and critical reflection was not part of their regular daily practices due to time constraints and often times unexpected interruptions that redirected their daily plans. Furthermore, overall teachers had concerns on the emphasis of the accountability testing framework in the state of Texas that seemed to draw attention and teaching time away from the critical lifelong learner skills students needed. As the work of the consultants was sustained, small group teacher sessions transitioned into learning communities and student assessment data provided a wealth of knowledge and insights into each individual campus. All information collected from administrators, teachers, and student data formulated a tentative plan for situated professional learning communities, for each individual campus. One interesting note was that while all four campuses shared some similar concerns and challenges, each campus requested varied forms of teacher support. The following narrative stories from teachers and administrators were provided voluntarily from the four campuses that received support.

# Teacher Narrative 1

The following teacher is a 7th grade Language Arts teacher who has been teaching Reading for 2 years and was transitioned into a Language Arts class for her 3rd year as a classroom teacher. During a series of meetings, with her campus administration and with the professional learning teacher sessions, it was clear that she had concerns because she felt that she had just begun the process of becoming comfortable with teaching Reading and had now been charged with teaching the writing process and teaching writing for communicative purposes. It is important to note that at the 7th grade, writing is assessed with a state test focused on expository writing and multiple choice questions focused on revising and editing reading passages at this grade level in the state of Texas. The novice teacher was anxious that she was not adequately prepared to assess writing much less comfortable with teaching writing. Administration requested weekly meetings with the 7th grade writing teachers and the consultant during the teachers' planning time as a way of supporting the four teachers. Each week teachers would reflect and engage in dialogue on their teaching strengths and share best practices amongst each other. When the teachers requested strategies or resources, the consultant would bring strategies and activities that could be easily introduced into their daily teaching and targeted objectives for that week. Three of the four writing teachers were veteran teachers that ranged from 5-10 years of teaching experience further on the trajectory path towards experienced teachers. The novice teacher in the group indicated that she struggled with teaching introductory paragraphs and with having students stay on the assigned writing topic. The consultant communicated the progression of the weekly meetings and recommended that instead of meeting weekly with the small groups of teachers that she would meet every other week with them and every other week she would conduct mini-teaching lessons/lesson demonstrations on topic focus and introductory paragraphs for the novice teacher.

The open lines of communication established an environment of trust where the administrative body and teacher were supportive of the assistance provided. Basically, the consultant was tasked with modeling certain strategies with the novice teacher's students, while the novice teacher observed the consultants' instruction and questioning while checking for student understanding. The consultant began with 30-minute teaching lessons and gradually decreased them to 15-minute modeling-teaching sessions. As the school semester progressed, the novice teacher became more comfortable with teaching topic focus and introductory paragraphs and then transitioned into being observed by the consultant as she taught and took command of her classroom instruction. The consultant continued to provide feedback and recommended that the novice teacher also take time to observe the other veteran teachers within her 7th grade group. The bi-monthly meetings with the 7th grade teachers provided opportunities for them to collaborate, connect, and support each other in the process. The 7th grade writing teachers formed professional communities of writers that evolved and that focused on various topics. The consultant at times was the provider of resources and at other times served as a facilitator for guiding the teachers towards becoming more reflective of their teaching practices within their classrooms. At the end of the support year, the novice teacher reported that she felt much more comfortable with teaching topic focus and introductory paragraphs, and writing in general, and more importantly she felt supported by her campus teachers and was looking forward to the next year to continue to build on the confidence she had developed from the support she had received.

## Teacher Narrative 2

The following 7th grade teacher of 10 years in the profession provided an account of her struggles with writing instruction and in preparing her students to become proficient writers that would be able to communicate effectively in the real world. The 7th grade teacher had taught

Language Arts (writing) during her time with the district and had knowledge of the changes on how writing instruction had changed over the years and how instruction had been greatly impacted by the stresses and challenges of state testing assessment in transitioning from a narrative descriptive essay focus to an expository focus. She felt equipped with effective strategies within the genres of both narrative and expository writing focus, but teaching grammar skills to students was always a challenge. The teacher described the majority of the student population of English language learners who were still transitioning into becoming proficient speakers and writers of the English language. The teacher indicated that 95% of her students were bilingual students whose first language was Spanish, and second language was English. This brought on challenges regarding writing in the second language which was English. Consistent grammar errors in student writing distracted from students' communicative goals at times. The noted patterns of errors signaled evidence of the transition from the native language to the second language which was evident as both languages had varying grammatical rules and did not necessary apply from one language to the other. The teacher had requested support with this focus on grammar instruction and in assisting her second language learners in the process. She also requested assistance with editing strategies. The other 7th teachers within her grade level (4 in all) and including 6th grade Reading teachers all voiced the same concerns regarding the progress of the student population of second language learners. Two consultants worked with this campus inclusive of 7th grade writing teachers and 6th grade Reading teachers. The two consultants met to conduct the needs assessments for both grade levels and content areas. While Reading and Writing were taught separately the consultants made every effort to assist the teachers in approaching both subjects as reciprocal areas of instruction that could build on each other. The first 4 weeks of meetings with both groups of teachers established the tone and set up the learning communities' basis. The grant also purchased and provided classroom sets of textbooks from the assigned reading school lists for 6th graders in efforts to reinforce reading in the English language. The campus had sets of classroom books, but they were dated, and students and teachers welcomed the new sets of books at their campus. The teachers were then each assigned one consultant for all 6th grade Reading teachers and one for all 7th grade English Language Arts teachers. The English Language Arts consultant gathered strategies on teaching grammar skills specifically targeting English language learners and modeled editing strategies within the context of teacher and student writing samples. The consultant emphasized the importance of providing grammatical instructional approaches within their own writing and avoided teaching grammar rules in isolation. Exposure to written essays in English also provided support for English language learners who required exposure to English regularly in efforts to understand and gain command of the English language. Both consultants began sharing best practices with teachers on a weekly basis during planning time. This included both Reading and Writing teachers; at times they met separately, at other times that met collaboratively. Teachers appreciated this connective time together. These meetings allowed opportunities for teachers in both areas to see how Reading and Writing instruction could serve as reciprocal processes that reinforce each other. As the learning communities evolved over a three month period, teachers were gradually implementing what had been shared and learned in the brief learning sessions. The teacher identified in this narrative had requested that the writing consultant model how to edit a teacher written essay in front of her classroom. The consultant began to serve as a coach and mentor and gradually conducted modeling sessions on editing, inclusive of teacher and student sample essays. The consultant relied on think aloud models where she would read a paragraph and asks students, "Does this sound correct?" "Could this sentence be rewritten to better communicate?" This think aloud protocol focused on metacognitive processes and provided students opportunities to think about their writing and how it can be improved to communicate better the message at hand. The consultant continued modeling for the students on a weekly basis using student essays and drafts. She gradually transitioned the think aloud teaching to the teacher and provided feedback and guidance as the consultant then observed the teacher. After the semester progressed, the consultants continued to develop the learning communities of teachers, but as they transitioned into the semester of state testing, they also added in small group student support sessions. The consultants worked with small group student pullout sessions with struggling writers who had limited command of the English language. These small group pull out sessions with students reinforced, supported, and extended on the instructional undertakings of the classroom teacher. The teacher in this narrative described the weekly consultant sessions of best practices and sharing, the consultant providing coaching and modeling of this teaching approach, and finally students were receiving individual small group instructional support. The combined efforts of support provided a safety net of confidence and sustainability where the teacher began to see her students improve in their writing in regard to grammar and communicating more effectively through their writing.

## Teacher Narrative 3

The following teacher was a 6th grade Reading teacher with 2 years of teaching experience. Administrators at this campus had requested mentoring and coaching sessions with the novice teacher during her planning time. The novice teacher was hesitant at first; but once she began working with the consultant, she experienced and appreciated being respected as an equal contributor in the process. The consultant began the once-a-week meetings as opportunities to development a professional relationship of trust and engaged dialogue where the teacher had opportunities to share her concerns and anxiety of being a novice teacher. The consultant provided the Reading teacher strategies on classroom management and real life examples on how to manage student behavior. These conversations really benefited the novice teacher as she described in her narrative responses. She progressively began to incorporate these classroom management strategies into her classroom, and she began to see a difference in student response behavior. After 4 sessions during the teacher's planning time, the consultant transitioned into providing whole classroom lesson demonstrations and modeling instructional strategies on building vocabulary. The novice teacher had concerns about students' vocabulary levels and the need to provide additional support for building comprehension through expanding their vocabulary. The lesson demonstrations began at 30-minutes per session, then reduced to 15-minute demonstrations, and then the novice teacher traded roles and was being observed by the consultant on vocabulary instruction. The feedback during these sessions by the consultant was described as invaluable by the novice teacher. This mentoring and coaching process transpired over a 3-month period. The novice teacher specifically noted that the vocabulary novel lessons and the vocabulary card strategy were the most beneficial and engaging for students. The novice teacher acknowledged that classroom management had improved and that allowed her to become a more effective and strategic teacher. The consultant returned the following semester to follow up with the novice teacher and to continue to provide any additional assistance. The progress was positive and encouraging, and the novice teacher expressed her gratitude for all the support provided as she still recognized that she was a work in progress.

## Administrator Narrative 4

The following administrator worked as a curriculum professional for a middle school campus for four years and a classroom teacher for eight years. The curriculum professional worked collaboratively with the consultants early at the start of the semester to reexamine how the structural organization of 6th-8th grade Reading and Language Arts teachers were organized and grouped. The curriculum professional provided background knowledge of the teachers, including years and levels of teaching experience, which was helpful for the consultants. The initial plan of action was to meet with the teachers in small groups by individual grade levels. Brief meetings with individual grade levels gave the teachers an opportunity to engage in reflective dialogue regarding the strengths and challenges in the classroom and to understand the needs of the students. Teachers appreciated these brief meetings as it provided them an opportunity to have their voices heard and their input valued in this process of curriculum mapping and planning. These professional learning communities' sessions then transitioned into brief meetings on assessing student writing and rubric scoring inclusive of all writing teachers. Several sessions on scoring, essay calibration and understanding how students were being assessed at the state level allowed teachers in collaboration with the curriculum professional and administrators to plan accordingly. The process of reviewing students' essays collaboratively provided insights into the strengths and weakness of students' writing abilities in grades 6th -7th. Teachers worked with consultants to include informal student samples as part of the conversation for the means of determining patterns and trends in student writing by reviewing formal and informal writing pieces. This valuable student assessment data and reflective dialogue among teachers, administrators, and consultants established a tentative plan to begin brief lesson demonstrations with teachers (15- 30 minutes) and provide teachers with strategies and external resources aligned with their curriculum sequence plan in the areas of writing instruction. Reading teachers were also included in the short demonstration meetings and as a means of supporting the writing teachers during their instruction of reading. Requests for classroom sets of novels designated by the school district reading lists were also honored and provided to the reading teachers. Consultants were asked to provide brief coaching and co-teaching of mini-lessons to novice and first year teachers in need of additional support. Veteran teachers at this campus also participated by sharing their best practices throughout this process during the professional learning sessions. Both the curriculum professional and the campus administrator were actively involved in overseeing the progress and adjustments were implemented based on student assessments. Overall, the curriculum professional was the driving force and primary support base behind this collaboration, and her willingness to include all stakeholders and value teacher input was important throughout the process. Challenges and setbacks occurred, but the curriculum professional remained focus and optimistic throughout the year. The curriculum professional was motivated and inspired by the benefits of the ongoing collaboration of these evolving learning communities and anticipated replicating this process in years to come.

## Teacher Narrative 5

As a Language Arts teacher of 11 years teaching 7th grade writing, she felt comfortable with teaching writing, but was challenged with the current situation of assisting her second language learner population of Spanish speakers with writing instruction. The teacher described herself as a veteran teacher and was happy to assist novice teachers and the rest of the campus staff when called upon. She was a leader at her campus and was often designated to lead teacher meetings that were developed and led by campus administration. This campus made it a priority to meet regularly and connect regarding curriculum concerns. These established communities at this campus had already begun the process of campus needs assessment and provided consultants with the data during the initial meetings. The professional learning groups were inclusive of Language Arts and Reading teachers and at varying times they met collaboratively and at other times they met separately by content areas. Three consultants were assigned to this campus and worked in different capacities at the request of the administrators and campus leaders. The consultants introduced the SEE-I model developed by Gerald M. Nosich (2009) to the Language Arts teachers. The consultants had utilized this framework for writing instruction and recommended it as a means of assisting students in developing their writing, specifically as a chunking technique for teaching writing development that would benefit second language learners, but also benefit all students collectively. SEE-I stands for state, elaborate, exemplify, and illustrate which establishes a framework for problem solving and critical thinking that provided a strategic approach to developing the writing process. This explicit and guided instructional approach was modeled by the consultants through small group sessions and modeling demonstrations. The veteran teacher described in this narrative would take the lead in with working with the consultants to provide support to other campus teachers. At times the consultants would assist the teachers when teaching each of the areas of the framework that students struggled with (co-teaching); at other times the consultants refrained and allowed teachers to experiment with the framework. The veteran teacher noted that she strongly supported this approach because she began to see immediate positive response from her students, especially the Spanish speaking population of students. Her weekly meetings with the teachers and consultants provided additional positive commentary on this approach. Overall, the in-class support the consultants provided in co-teaching and modeling this pedagogical approach was extremely beneficial for all teachers and more importantly proved effective in assisting our students.

## Conclusions

The randomly selected response narratives provided by the educators and administrators are an indication that all schools differ and that all were at different trajectory levels in their careers. It is evident by the responses that differentiated professional learning communities and all stakeholders working collaboratively in engaged consistent dialogue alongside teacher support can have a positive impact. Change takes time. Gradual change, in some cases transformational change, occurred at some of these middle schools at an ongoing pace over a three-year period at varied levels with consultants facilitating the progression. Of the four middle school campuses, participation into the grant varied with some campuses receiving a few targeted professional development sessions based on student needs assessment, while other campuses received mentoring, coaching, modeling, co-teaching, mini-lesson demonstrations, and targeted small group student focused instruction. All in all, consultants conducted varied work at various times at these campuses. These narratives here are an indication of stakeholders working collaboratively to find solutions to the challenges that were currently in place at their designated campus in efforts to better assist students. Risko and Vogt (2016) refer to this process as teachers engaging in professional learning in action and through an inquiry approach process. The inquiry process took on different forms based on the campus needs and requests. Consultants worked to validate teachers' voices and focused on their inclusion of campus curricular decisions. According to Mezirow's (1991) theory of transformational learning, transformation can lead to more inclusive, reflective discourse, differentiated and integrated perspective towards development of self. The work conducted by the consultants with the educators indicated clear signs of reflection of content which is important, but clearly evidence of critical and reflective discourse was apparent as teachers engaged in these differentiated learning communities within their campuses. Senge et al.(2012) suggests that in order to improve a school system it must transition into a learning school that reflects on how educators think and how they interact with each other. The consultants, as part of this grant initiative, attempted to engage educators and administrators in this process through differentiated learning communities within each campus.

## Questions for Deeper Reflective Action

1) The research informs us that teacher support and working collaboratively are critical to the success of any school campus. What are your thoughts about the research and the actual school/classroom practices not always being in alignment with one another?

2) Reflect on the educator and administrator narrative responses provided here in this chapter. What are your experiences with teacher support services that you can identify with, as described in the narratives provided.

3) Including all stakeholders in the process when forming professional learning communities is important. Identifying both student and teacher strengths and weakness are the foundations for establishing pathways and goals for moving forward. How do you envision your campus establishing these foundations in putting forth professional learning communities?

## Responses:

# Chapter IV: Authentic Lessons Learned from Professional Learning Communities in Action

The three-year grant initiative began on the premise of the Write for Texas principles aligned with the National Writing Project Model. The principles of the grant project included: using writing and reading to support student learning in other content areas, teaching students the thinking processes and skills necessary to communicate effectively through writing and provide varied strategies for the improvement of writing instruction while providing additional assistance and support for struggling writers. These guiding principles were supported by the establishment of professional learning communities. As for the National Writing Project, their model is focused on teachers teaching teachers and working collaboratively on sustained efforts to improve writing and learning for all learners. This includes identifying and developing teacher and educator leaders, providing support for educators in their local service areas, and providing professional learning communities for educators' continued learning. These combined established principles for our team in South Texas were the primary overall goals to develop differentiated professional learning communities within each priority designated campus and support teachers in the areas of reading, writing, and critical thinking. Our entire team of consultants (18 coaches) and support staff were optimistic and motivated to work on this project which began as a pilot program in 2014-2015. The number of operational consultants gradually decreased over time due to attrition. This included some consultants conducting work in designated school districts in nearby surrounding towns; however, only survey respondents at the four designated middle schools were included and reflected here. All consultants were eager to support teachers in the areas of reading and writing, as all consultants had worked within the public school systems in some capacity over the years and understood the challenges teachers encountered on a regular basis. The compassion, drive, and dedication of those individuals involved in the project were inspiring. The unique nature of this project was the juxtaposition of having guiding principles and goals, but not really having a plan. By this I mean we were not aware how the school district or the priority designated schools would respond. At the onset, we did not know what types of services or how I would organize the requests for teacher support demands. As the administrator of this collective project alongside a strong leadership team, we evolved into our own professional learning community team. After initial meetings with district leaders, campus administrators, and teachers the project tasks became more defined based on the communications with the specific campuses. Thereafter, I was able to develop schedules outlining various teacher support tasks which were adjusted and modified and flexible. As we spent more time with campus educators, the project evolved into what each campus had uniquely envisioned. As previously mentioned, some campuses requested extensive teacher support and resources; while, others requested limited support and resources. Our team respected the request of each individual campus, even when we saw areas that we could contribute to; we were respectful of the leadership and hardworking educators in each campus. The other unique nature of this project is that we had a state wide support base of educators and leaders in different capacities across the state of Texas that were also embarking in the same journey we were undertaking. A combined total of 20 Education Service Centers and 7 National Writing Project sites (27 entities in all) across Texas were provided grant funding all in efforts to support teachers across the state. During the initial inception of this project in 2014-2015, consultants (coaches) across the state serviced 153 schools and by the conclusion of the project 198 schools had been serviced across the state of Texas. The network of support from this grant included state leadership meetings, consistent on-line meetings, sharing of ideas and strategies through various platforms including a website resource for coaches and educators as part of the grant.

As a team we started this journey, we had high hopes for success of the project, but we were also not sure, how or if, this would work or what the outcome would be. Our vision as a team was that we would establish professional learning communities that would evolve and maintain sustainability over time and the work conducted would have a positive impact on the student and on academic performance long term.

The overall findings on the grant project across the state of Texas reported positive results and feedback from consultants and teachers involved in the initiative. Different sites across Texas engaged in a variety of approaches at varying levels; and each site highlighted different areas of focus which included the development of reflective dialogic respectful trusting relationships with peers, integrated modeling and co-teaching routines as a means of teacher support, and one significant achievement noted was institutional and individual professional growth. The opportunities for consultants (coaches) to work collaboratively alongside administrators, educators, and students were invaluable and set the ground work for this phenomenon to occur. Positive changes in academic student performance were also recognized in the report at various sites across the state as well.

This grant project in the South Texas region provided engagement, opportunities, and awareness of the challenges that administrators and educators encountered locally and statewide on a daily basis within their respective classrooms. The 3-year project sheds light on the potential and the hard working educators and administrators that encompass the priority district we were fortunate to work with. All participants were asked to complete a survey at the termination of the three-year grant. The grant project educators and administrators were asked to provide feedback on a voluntarily basis on the services they received at their campus. Due to the differentiated support that was offered, it was a challenge to attempt to quantify different variables evolving at different trajectory levels. Lent (2007) as mentioned previously, discusses how engagement in professional learning communities is not easily measured with immediate data as they are evolving living entities that vary by campus and district and measurability varies and occurs over time. This is often the deterrent factor of many school districts' unwillingness to participate in learning communities in that they are not easily measured with quantified data immediately.

The survey responses provided by educators at the end of the three-years provided qualitative narratives of their experiences through their participation in the initiative. This included descriptions of the most beneficial support services, the most effective instructional strategies/techniques learned, and the challenges encountered along the way. In addition, the team of consultants and staff reviewed and evaluated overall student academic performances based on state assessment exams in the areas of Reading and Writing. Student sample essays were also an area of focus specifically because of the extensive nature of the writing instructional support services that were provided. As previously mentioned, change takes time, if it is to be impactful and meaningful.

## Lessons Learned: Support Services

The educator and administrator participants were asked specifically to list and describe the types of services they received from the grant project and which were the most impactful, if at all, or beneficial in the form of teacher support. Of those that responded, 100% of all respondents that completed the surveys commented on coaching and mentoring services as being the most meaningful in terms of teacher support. Some respondents shared additional commentary that consultants served as excellent mentors and coaches (facilitators) that led the learning communities meetings and carved out time during the busy week to engage them in meaningful conversations where their voices mattered, and they had opportunities to discuss curricular concerns. Some

56

respondents commented that having their voices heard was not common practice at some campuses. A few novice teachers also commented how they learned about more effective classroom management strategies through some of their mentoring sessions. Overall, coaching and mentoring were significantly the highest rated and commented category of support that educators and administrators seemed to value the most and asserted that they felt was meaningful in regard to teacher support.

The second category most commented on by survey respondents was co-teaching and modeling instructional practices or strategies. Educators and administrators alike were aligned in terms of their favorable responses regarding this support service. Educators specifically described how the consultants (coaches), engaged their students with specific strategies targeting areas that teachers themselves had requested because they did not feel confident teaching in that subject matter area. The modeling of instructional strategies, as one 7th grade teacher described, "made me more aware of how to break down content material (scaffold for students)" so students would better understand including "multiple ways of explaining the same concept through hands-on activities that proved more meaningful." This coincides with multiple statements made by respondents in regard to modeling support services. Veteran teachers also provided commentary regarding the co-teaching as they really appreciated the opportunity to bring in master teachers (consultants) to share the teaching stage and learn from each other in the process. Furthermore, some teachers even commented on how they envision themselves engaging in more co-teaching amongst their own campus peers. All in all, the comments collectively by the respondents identified incremental levels of instructional academic impact through their informal assessments of their students based on these support services.

The third most commented category as per respondents was the small group student instruction. Respondents referred to this service as small group pullout sessions or small group interventions and others viewed them as small group Reading/Writing workshops. These services were conducted at the request of educators and administrators and were designed as an extension of the coaching and modeling of strategies sessions within the learning communities. Survey respondents expressed that the targeted small group instruction was extremely beneficial for all, but particularly for those students that were second-language learners that required additional support. They also expressed in their commentaries that they really appreciated this support as they sometimes felt that with large classrooms of students, they were not always able to provide this individualized instruction and follow up that the consultants were able to provide.

## Lessons Learned: Pedagogical Practices and Strategies

The survey respondents were asked to list or describe specific instructional practices, approaches, strategies, or techniques that they embraced and integrated into their daily practice. Some of the Reading strategies mentioned by educators included graphic organizers, think aloud strategies for comprehension, vocabulary card games, and writing to learn lesson ideas based on assigned novels. Educators commented on the variety of graphic organizers as part of the support resources that were shared with teachers including character and sequencing of story events that were beneficial for students. In addition, the "writing to learn" lesson ideas assisted students with comprehension. They served as effective informal writing activities that allowed students' opportunities to work through sequence of events in novels. The survey respondents specifically commented on the think aloud comprehension strategies and their effectiveness on student understanding of events. The think aloud sessions occurred in some instances during whole class modeling sessions and in other instances during educator modeling group sessions (mini-professional development sessions) during the professional learning community meetings.

Survey respondents commented on the pedagogical practices of engagement with regards to better understanding state writing assessment rubrics and scoring. Consultants, at the request of some campuses, were asked to participate in multiple learning community sessions where educators including administrators would assess student writing, engage in essay calibration discussions, and dialogue about the weakness and strengths in student writing. These conversations proved that all stakeholders involved had a vested interest in understanding what the state expectations were, but more importantly in understanding student needs. This practice was highly praised by some respondents who participated in this process.

With regards to specific instructional practices for writing, survey respondents mentioned a variety of strategies in their commentary remarks that were modeled and shared as best practices during their sessions. Some of the repeated strategies that were integrated in daily practice included: admit and exit slips, quick writes, and Kelly Gallagher's (2011) real-world writing purposes (Appendix A), as well as using mentor texts. Alongside these strategies, the most impactful on student writing, as outlined by educators, was the SEE-I model that was documented in one of the previous teacher narratives. The SEE-I model was well received and requested by educators who were optimistic that this approach would really benefit students, targeting second-language learners, but beneficial to all students. Once introduced to this approach educators requested more specific training and modeling on this process. SEE-I which stands for state, elaborate, exemplify, illustrate is a framework for facilitating the premise for problem-solving and critical thinking strategies situated in the teaching of the writing process.

The consultants (coaches) utilized the framework by Nosich (2009) and Paul & Elder (2010) which established the premise for how this approach could be implemented in efforts to improve the quality of student's thinking and writing processes. Extensive research on secondary writing (Graham & Perin, 2007; Persky, Daane, & Ying, 2003; Granham, Gillespie, McKeown, 2013) reminds educators that writing is not only a complex process, but one that students struggle with and require extensive practice in. This explicit and guided approach was a tool for body paragraph development that required thinking through ideas and all the while building on more ideas that allowed for effective communication and clarity, making abstract concepts concrete through their writing. SEE-I was a mechanism for working through the writing process by reasoning through a statement (thesis), then elaborating or explaining the statement, then working through examples that would clarify meaning, and finally an illustration that would showcase and capture a true image of the meaning of the ideas through an analogy or comparison. The consultants, engaged in this implementation process deserve immeasurable credit and validation for the hard work and dedication that was put forth in the visuals, charts, and mentor text examples provided as part of the SEE-I model (Appendix B). A group of consultants worked collaboratively and reviewed student essays on a regular basis throughout the grant program and at the end of the project to determine any significant impact on student writing performance. Additional details and research on consultant engagement and implementation of this specific SEE-I framework is outlined in a research article in *The Journal of Middle Level Education in Texas* (Spring 2019). Upon review of multiple student essays over the 3-year initiative cycle, there were gradual changes in student writing that became evident after extensive review. There were clear signs of more cohesiveness, clarity, and development that became more consistent from the first year to the final year of the project. The following snap shots of randomly selected student writing samples showcase patterns of the evolution and development of student writing. The first set of Sample Student Essays #1 & #2 provided below are derived from the implementation year of the grant. The second set of Sample Student Essays #1 & #2 provided below are derived from the concluding year of the grant. The randomly selected essays were writing samples from students at the designated campuses receiving extensive support services from the grant initiative.

**Sample Student Essay #1 Implementation Year**

What is the importance of having a good friend?
The importance of having a good friend is a blessing because taked part of your family.
Always stayed with you, cared one to another, never fight. Sometimes had ploblems, but always resolued that problems together.
In sometimes the problems wes not given in the friendship, was in the street, park, or in our family, but always your friend was in the school, or in our home, for talked that problem with her, and resolued that problem for example, my friend walked in the street directed to his house, but a car stoped, and taked away her phone, then my friend and I resolued that problem
However, with a good friend you can go to their house, park, see movies, to the Mall go shopping, or in sometimes go to a fieldtrip with a friend. The good friend although give advice with any problem you have, but not is on a problem although can be use on a secret, or a simple advice that you need about a person that you like.
I conclude that "A friend is a gift you give youself."

**Sample Student Essay #2 Implementation Year**

Having a good friend ship with Someone is not that easy, well if it is easy he or her are just friends not a good friend Cause a good friend are people you can chrust they will alway be there to talk to if you have a problem, and if you tell them your secrets they won't tell now one does friend are good Some friends if you tell them they tell everyone does arn't good friends you want to trust friends come and go. But best friend don't cause not a lot of people are like that good friends are cool. Caus they can have your back you can count on them, they can saport you help you up with stuff that you don't know push you to your liment does are stuff that a true friend is.

"If you can dream it, you can achive it," -Lisa and Lena. Nothing worth having comes easy. The only way you'll get what you want is by setting a goal for it.

When you set a goal you can invision yourself or whatever it must be and think of ways to reach it. It is important to set a goal cause if not you wont know what to do. When you set a goal It makes it easier to accomplish something caus you already know what your aiming for. You can set mini goals to reach for the big one.

Also, by setting a goal, it helps you prepare. It gives the oppertonity to find ways to reach it and to work hard for it. Before reach the goal there must be little goals to help get the main price. I helps us work harder each time.

You must try your best to better your good utill your good is better and your better is best. Nothing goes to you, you have to go to it. I think the most important part abos setting is that it helps you keep your eyes on the price.

**Sample Student Essay #2 Concluding Year**

It's important to set a goal in advance because you're think about your future. You will think smarter and be faster. You will achieve your goals that you've set for yourself.

To begin with, many people set future goals for themselves and so should you. Many people say that after high school they will go to college. They set a future goal. In order to go to college you need to get good grades in high school. That's why people should think smarter. For example, my brother Josh set himself a goal that after college, he will become a firefighter. He was struggling with things in college. So, he dropped out and didn't reach his goal. He didn't think that he was gonna be able to do it and he gave. Some people do achieve their goals, For instance my sister Diana was very intelligent and she wanted to be a doctor. She went on to be a doctor and she was happy for reaching her goal.

In conclusion, setting advance goals can help you conquer your dreams and it will all be worth it.

It is evident from these randomly selected samples that student writing development evolved and had encompassed more examples and clarity in the process over time. While it is important to note that positive changes in student writing development occurred, this was not immediately transferrable to state accountability testing measure outcomes for all four campuses. However, on a positive note, in an overview of the state assessment writing performance scores during the three-year grant project, two of the designated campuses identified and reported gradual consistent increases on student writing performance in each of the three-years. All campuses are to be commended for their hard work and engagement in support services and resources from the grant project site. The SEE-I model within the learning communities framework proved to be an impactful learned strategy that educators would continue to use and adapt for future use as noted in their survey responses.

## Lessons Learned: Challenges Encountered

While extensive positive outcomes have been outlined by the survey respondents, the challenges encountered must also be included in this authentication of lessons learned. School systems across the country struggle with accountability high stakes assessment testing, and South Texas is no different from other states in comparison in regard to accountability standards. The large population of second-language learners, at the designated priority school district, also presented another variable of importance for the need for differentiated instruction that would assist all students. One of the challenges encountered in this journey was the overwhelming emphasis on district and campus focus on state testing accountability. It is highly understandable that school district administrative bodies are accountable to the expectations of the high stakes testing in Texas; and these are the lenses from which they view, conduct daily practice, and make decisions that tie into this accountability factor district wide. At times throughout the three-year process of this initiative, the team of consultants found themselves being asked to teach to the test or test strategies. Consultants found this position challenging and made efforts to work with teachers and administration to highlight the importance of instructional strategies with the goal of creating lifelong learners and that the instructional strategies provided would assist the students in being successful in meeting state accountability measures. Some days our team of consultants won these ongoing struggles, other days our team found themselves surrendering to the campuses that we were committed to provide support. The challenge was that at times administrators and teachers had different goals for students, and this was the misalignment. The encouraging factor was that all stakeholders involved wanted students to succeed; the challenge was differences on the pathway to arriving there. The challenges we observed and encountered throughout the duration of the grant are consistent with research conducted by Lent (2007) in that in the formation and work conducted in developing professional learning communities sometimes we can "get lost in accountability shuffle" (p. 10) and that becomes priority. Furthermore, our team of consultants also endured some challenges as we began with a large network of 18 consultants and gradually that number decreased due to work demands and family responsibilities and commitments from our consultants. But as a team, we worked through these challenges and continued to schedule support services as requested and as best as we could.

Another challenge encountered and observed during the process, was as a team we found ourselves working towards creating a balance and mediating between administration and educators. At times, brief meetings by administration were requested; and at other times collaborative meetings with all educators and consultants were requested. At times this was deemed as necessary, but at other times it was important to bring everyone together and build on the trust factor to fully embrace and establish the groundwork for learning communities. Both educators and administrators sometimes found themselves not engaging in conversations or not effectively communicating even when they found themselves in close proximity of each other. Trust and conversations amongst educators and between educators and administration are crucial to the success of any school campus. As a team we worked collaboratively with all stakeholders and envisioned learning communities of trust where teachers were included in the decision making process regarding curricular issues at hand. All these challenges were part of the on-going process and as a project we made efforts to develop and establish strong learning communities that were inclusive and respectful of all the expertise within the groups. These observed behaviors might seem odd, but the truth of the matter is schools are high level functioning entities constantly actively engaged in time constraint environments that prevent ongoing regular communications and can lead to distrust and create environments not conducive to student learning. Senge (2006) describes building shared visions and team learning as part of learning organizations disciplines for success. Senge (2006) asserts that a shared vision by an organization is where all entities excel and learn, but the challenge is translating each individual goal into a shared vision then this is where team learning and thinking together coincide. This is the difference between meeting sessions and professional learning communities, and as a team, our expectations were to assist in facilitating these learning communities with a shared vision.

Upon reflecting on the grant project on the local level and state wide, it is without a doubt that individuals invested in improving education are hardworking, dedicated, and passionate. The statewide network provided a supportive foundation so each site could collaborate, network, share ideas; and it was through these professional learning communities at the state level that provided a foundation for the team administrators and consultants (coaches) to organize and implement the pedagogical practices for the priority designated schools across the state. At the inception of the grant, our overall combined shared vision and goals for our team in South Texas were to develop differentiated professional learning communities within each priority designated campus and support teachers in the areas of reading, writing, and critical thinking. Challenges were encountered, teacher turnover was a factor; miscommunications occurred, adjustments were made, flexibility was key, mediation was practiced, but the unyielding commitment of all stakeholders involved stayed committed to the improvement of student success. Lessons were learned along the way. Reflection and dialogue become a gradual occurrence as a part of the campus culture. Viewing teaching as a craft and with a growth mind set, a school of learning can transform into a learning school. Based on participant feedback, observations, and triangulation of information collected the project was deemed successful, impactful, and meaningful. The following commentary provided by a teacher respondent, as she quoted her student, provides a student perspective on what the focus of professional learning communities in school systems should be about- the development of lifelong learners:

> "I hated to write. Writing was painful. It was so hard," one student said. "However now my teachers seem to like writing and I feel differently now and realize writing can be fun and interesting... and I can now write about what I know.... and like"

This is evidence of transformational school change; change takes time, if it is to be impactful and meaningful, and it is not always measurable.

# Questions for Deeper Reflective Action

1) Extensive research supports the practice of teacher support services to avoid teacher fatigue and teacher burn-out. Describe your experiences with support services at your campus. What suggestions do you have as an educator/administrator in supporting teachers at your campus/district?
2) Describe your most impactful pedagogical practices or strategies utilized in the classroom. How do you envision yourself sharing your best practices with other teachers within your school campus?
3) School districts across the country encounter multiple challenges regarding accountability state testing measures to teacher isolation. What are the challenges at your campus that you feel impede teacher/administrator professional development and advancement?

# Responses:

# Conclusions

After 24 years in the field of education, I still find myself reflecting on and replicating the communities that inspired me growing up in South Texas. The communities we engage in throughout our lives are pieces of a puzzle that make up our unique self. The intended goal of this book was to provide a narrative account of the experiences of this three-year grant initiative. This goal also included providing teachers a voice and validation for the hard work they perform daily. My hope is that I have provided insights into how impactful community can be in the education of all students. All life experiences influence our communities, shape our lives, and influence our journeys. As educators, we have a responsibility to be disseminators of knowledge, but more importantly we have the power to impact lives. Teaching moments are those that do not come about often; and when they do, it is important to seize them and connect with our students. I am grateful to all participants of this grant initiative who have shared their expertise and have given of their time due to their commitment to education. I am also grateful and inspired by the school district administrators and teachers who participated in this initiative. I began with communities, and I will conclude with communities, I am encouraged that the foundations set forth regarding professional learning communities will continue to evolve in these schools and engage everyone in deeper reflection and conversations of those things that really matter... as learning is both personal and social, and it connects us (Senge et al., 2012).

# References

Aguilar, E. (2013). *The art of coaching: Effective strategies for school transformation.* San Francisco, CA: Jossey-Bass Co.

Annenberg Institute for School Reform. (2004). *Instructional coaching: Professional development strategies that improve instruction.* Providence, RI: Brown University. Retrieved from: www.annenberginstitute.org/pdf/InstructionalCoaching.pdf

Bandura, A. (1977). *Social learning theory.* New York, NY: General Learning Press.

Boreen, J., Johson, M., Niday, D.,& Potts, J. (2000). *Mentoring beginning teachers: Guiding, reflecting, coaching.* Portsmouth, NH: Stenhouse Publishers.

Brock, A. & Hundley, H. (2016). *The growth mindset coach.* Berkley, CA: Ulysses Press.

Chapman, D. (1983). A model of the influences on teacher retention. *Journal of Teacher Education, 34*(5), 43-49. *doi.org/10.1177/002248718303400512*

Darling-Hammond, L. & Richardson, N. (2009). Teacher learning, what matters. *Educational Leadership, ASCD, 66*(5), 45-53.

Darling-Hammond, L., Wei, R., Andree, A., Richardson, N., Orphanos, S. (2009). Professional learning in the learning profession: A status report on teacher development in the United States and abroad. Published by the *National Staff Development Council.*

Diez, M. (2007). Looking back and moving forward: Tensions in the teacher dispositions discourse. *Journal of Teacher Education, 58*(5), 388-396.

Dogan, S., Pringle, R. & Mesa, J. (2015). The impacts of professional learning communities on science teachers' knowledge, practice and student learning: A review. *Professional Development in Education, 42*(4), 569-588.

Dweck, C. (2008) *Mindset: The new psychology of success.* New York, NY: Ballantine Books.

Elbow, P. (1998). *Writing with power: Techniques for mastering the writing process* (2nd Ed.). New York, NY: Oxford University Press.

Gallagher, K. (2011) *Write like this: Teaching real-world writing through modeling and mentor texts.* Port, ME: Stenhouse.

Graham, S. & Perin, D. (2007). *Writing next: Effective strategies to improve writing of adolescents in middle and high schools.* A Report to Carnegie Corporation of New York. Washington, DC: Alliance for Excellent Education. Retrieved from: https://www.carnegie.org/media/filer_public/3c/f5/3cf58727-34f4-4140-a014-723a00ac56f7/ccny_report_2007_writing.pdf

Graham, S., Gillespie, A., McKeown, D. (2013). Writing importance development and instruction. *Reading and Writing: An Interdisciplinary Journal, 26* (1), 1-15.

Guha, R., Hyler, M., & Darling-Hammond, L. (2017). The teacher residency: A practical pathway to recruitment and retention. *American Educator, 41*(1), 31-44.

Hampton, K. (2010).Transforming school and society: Examining the theoretical foundations of scholar-practitioner leadership. *Scholar-Practitioner Quarterly, 4*(2), 185-193.

Hollins, E. R., McIntyre, L. R., DeBose, C., Hollins, K. S., &Towner, A. (2004). Promoting a self-sustaining learning community: Investigating an internal model for teacher development. *International Journal of Qualitative Studies in Education, 17*(2), 247–264.

Joyce, B. R., & Showers, B. (1985). Teachers coaching teachers. *Educational Leadership 42*(117): 38-43.

Joyce, B. R., & Showers, B. (2002). *Student achievement through staff development (3rd Ed.).* Alexandria, VA: Association for Supervision & Curriculum Development.

Koleman, J., Roegman, R. & Goodwin, L. (2017). Learner-centered mentoring: Building from student teachers individual needs and experiences as novice practitioners. *Teacher Education Quarterly, 44*(3), 93-117.

Kragler, S., Martin, L.E. & Sylvester, R. (2014). Lessons learned: What our history and research tell us about teachers' professional learning. In L.E. Martin, S. Kragler, D. J. Quatroche, & K.L. Bauserman (Eds.) *Handbook of professional development in education: Successful models and practices, Pre-K-12* (pp.483-505). New York, NY: Guilford.

Lee, V., Smith, J., & Croninger, R. (1995). Another look at high school restructuring. *Issues in Restructuring Schools (#9).* Madison, WI: Center on Organization and Restructuring of Schools.

Lent, R.C. (2007). *Literacy learning communities: A guide for creating sustainable change in secondary schools.* Portsmouth, NH: Heinemann.

Lomas, C., Hofman, R.H., & Bosker, R.J. (2011). Professional communities and student achievement meta-analysis. *School Effectiveness and School Improvement, 22* (2), 121-148. doi: 10.1080/09243453.2010.550467

Lumpe, A. (2007). Research-based professional development: Teachers engaged in professional learning communities, *Journal of Science Teacher Education,* 18(1), 125-128.

Margalef , L. & Roblin, R. (2016). Unpacking the roles of the facilitator in higher education professional learning communities, *Educational Research and Evaluation, 22* (3-4), 155-172. doi: 10.1080/13803611.2016.1247722

Marge, S. (2012). A conversation with Linda Darling-Hammond: The challenges of supporting new teachers. *Educational Leadership, 69*(8), 18-23.

Meier, D. (2002). *Schools we trust: Creating communities of learning in an era of testing and standardization*. Boston, MA: Beacon Press.

Merriam, S. (2004). The role of cognitive development in Mezirow's transformational learning theory. *Adult Education Quarterly, 55*(1), 60-68.

Mezirow, J. (1991). *Transformative dimensions of adult learning.* San Francisco, CA: Jossey-Bass Co.

Mezirow, J. (1998). On critical reflection. *Adult Education Quarterly, 48*(3), 185-198. doi.org/10.1177/074171369804800305

Mezirow, J. & Associates. (2000). *Learning as transformation: Critical perspective on a theory in progress.* San Francisco, CA: Jossey-Bass Co.

Murray, T. & Sheninger, E. (2017). *Learning transformed: 8 keys to designing tomorrow's schools, today.* Alexandria, VA: Association for Supervision & Curriculum Development.

Newell, G., Koukis, S., & Boster, S., (2007). Best practices in developing writing across the curriculum program in secondary schools. In S. Graham, C. MacArthur, & J. Fitzgerald (Eds.) *Best Practices in Writing Instruction.* New York; NY: Guilford Press.

Nosich, G. M. (2005). Problems with two standard models for teaching critical thinking. *New Directions for Community Colleges*, 3 *(130), 59-67.*

Nosich, G. M. (2009). *Learning to think things through: A guide to critical thinking across the curriculum* (3rd Ed). Upper Saddle River, N.J: Pearson Publishers.

Odell, S. & Ferraro, D. (1992). Teacher mentoring and teacher retention. *Journal of Teacher Education. 43*(3), 200-214. doi.org/10.1177/0022487192043003006

Paul, R., & Elder, L. (2010). The Foundation for Critical Thinking: Universal Intellectual Standards. Retrieved from http://www.criticalthinking.org/pages/universal-intellectual-standards/527

Persky, H., Daane, M.,& Ying, J. (2003). The Nation's Report Card: Writing, 2002. Retrieved from http://www.nces.ed.gov/nationsreportcard.

Risko, V. & Vogt, M.E. (2016). *Professional learning in action: An inquiry based approach for teachers of literacy*. New York, NY: Teachers College Press.

Sanchez, B., Kazen, H. & Cantu, L. (2019). SEE-I critical thinking framework: Expository writing in the middle schools. *The Journal of Middle Level Education in Texas. 6* (1).

Scherer, M. (2012). A conversation with Linda Darling-Hammond: The challenges of supporting new teachers. *Educational Leadership, 69*(8), 18-23.

Senge, P. (2006). *The fifth discipline: The art and practice of the learning organization.* New York, NY: Currency Publishing.

Senge, P., Cambron-McCabe, N., Lucas, T., Smith, B., Dutton, J., & Kleiner, A. (2012). *Schools that learn (Updated and Revised): A fifth discipline field book for educators, parents, and everyone who cares about education.* New York, NY: Crown Business Publishing.

Sparks, D. (2001). Why change is so challenging for schools: An interview with Peter Senge. *Journal of Staff Development, 22* (3), 42-47.

Sparks, D. (2002). *Designing powerful professional development for teachers and principals.* Oxford, OH: National Staff Development Council.

Strauss, V. (2013, April 11). What teachers need and reformers ignore: Time to collaborate. *The Washington Post.* Retrieved from: https://www.washingtonpost.com/news/answer-sheet/wp/2013/04/11/what-teachers-need-and-reformers-ignore-time-to-collaborate/?noredirect=on&utm_term=.6bc47edb9fde

Styron, R., & Styron, J. (2011). Critical issues facing school principals. *Journal of College Teaching and Learning, 8*(5), 1-10.

Taylor, E. (2007). An update of transformative learning theory: A critical review of the empirical research (1999-2005), *International Journal of Lifelong Learning, 26*, 173-191.

The Foundation for Critical Thinking. (2018). Retrieved from: http://www.criticalthinking.org/pages/critical-thinking-where-to-begin/796.

Vescio, V, Ross, D., & Alyson, A. (2008). Review of research on the impact of professional learning communities on teaching practice and student learning. *Teaching and Teacher Education: An International Journal of Research and Studies, 24*(1), 80-91.

White, S, & Mindell, N. R. (2014). Creating a transformational learning experience: Immersing students in an intensive interdisciplinary learning environment. *International Journal for the Scholarship of Teaching and Learning, 8* (2). doi.org/10.20429/ijsotl.2014.080203

Write for Texas Report. (2018). *Success stories from a literacy initiative* (2014-2017).

# Appendix A

# Real-World Writing Purposes

| Purpose | Explanation |
|---|---|
| **express and reflect** | The writer…<br>…expresses or reflects on his or her own life and experiences.<br>…often looks backwards in order to look forward. |
| **inform and explain** | The writer…<br>…states a main point and purpose.<br>…tries to present the information in a surprising way. |
| **evaluate and judge** | The writer…<br>…focuses on the worth of person, object, idea, or other phenomenon.<br>…usually specifies the criteria to the object being seen as "good" or "bad." |
| **inquire and explore** | The writer…<br>…wrestles with a question or problem.<br>…hooks with the problem and lets the reader watch them wrestle with it. |
| **analyze and interpret** | The writer…<br>…seeks to analyze and interpret on phenomena that are difficult to understand or explain. |
| **take a stand/ propose a solution** | The writer…<br>…seeks to persuade audiences to accept a particular position on a controversial issue.<br>…describes the problem, proposes a solution, and provides justification. |

Source: adapted from Reading Rhetorically, by Bean, Chappell, and Gillam.

Gallagher, K. (2011) *Write like this: Teaching real-world writing through modeling and mentor texts.* Port, ME: Stenhouse.

**S**tate the first reason that supports your thesis statement. Now circle your KEY word(s).

_____
_____
_____
_____
_____

**E**laborate your reason by using **different words** or **synonyms** for the key words above to **explain** and clarify what your statement means. Start your sentence with:

In other words,　　OR　　This means　　OR　　Put another way,　OR
To build on this idea　OR　　To clarify　　OR　　To extend on this idea
Be sure to include **synonyms** for the **KEY words** in your statement. Circle them!

_____
_____
_____
_____
_____
_____

**E**xemplify your reason by creating a SPECIFIC example that is "married" to your KEY words above. Add details that help your reader "see" your reason by answering the questions:

Who?
What?
Why?
When?
How?

You may start your sentence with:

For example,
OR
For instance,
OR
One time,

Circle **key words/phrases**! Check to see that you're still "married" to your main reason.

_____
_____
_____
_____
_____

**I**llustrate your reason by thinking like a **genius**! Create an analogy (a comparison, simile, or metaphor) that helps your reader "see" your reason. Be sure to circle **key words/phrases**!
**It's like...**

_____
_____
_____

Nosich, G. M. (2009). *Learning to think things through: A guide to critical thinking across the curriculum (*3rd Ed). Upper Saddle River, N.J: Pearson Publishers. 33-38.

Sanchez, B., Kazen, H. & Cantu, L. (2019). SEE-I critical thinking framework: Expository writing in the middle schools. *The Journal of Middle Level Education in Texas. 6* (1).